To
Amy

MW00907796

Thank You so much
for supporting. Can't
wait to purchase yours!!

-Ondonna
Sgt

2·2020

A Memoir of Conversations
between a Black Mother and her Daughter

CONVERSATIONS WITH MOM

Ordonna R. Sargeant, PMP

Copyright © 2019 Ordonna R. Sargeant, PMP.

All rights reserved. No part of this book may be reproduced, stored, or transmitted by any means—whether auditory, graphic, mechanical, or electronic—without written permission of the author, except in the case of brief excerpts used in critical articles and reviews. Unauthorized reproduction of any part of this work is illegal and is punishable by law.

This book is a work of non-fiction. Unless otherwise noted, the author and the publisher make no explicit guarantees as to the accuracy of the information contained in this book and in some cases, names of people and places have been altered to protect their privacy.

ISBN: 978-1-6847-1377-6 (sc)
ISBN: 978-1-6847-1376-9 (e)

Because of the dynamic nature of the Internet, any web addresses or links contained in this book may have changed since publication and may no longer be valid. The views expressed in this work are solely those of the author and do not necessarily reflect the views of the publisher, and the publisher hereby disclaims any responsibility for them.

Any people depicted in stock imagery provided by Getty Images are models, and such images are being used for illustrative purposes only. Certain stock imagery © Getty Images.

Interior Image Credit: Cory Sargeant

Lulu Publishing Services rev. date: 01/08/2020

CONTENTS

CAREER TALKS

DEDICATION

To MY MOTHER DENISE, who's wisdom and love made this possible and my children, Adriana, and Ava, be your best, do your best and live your best life.

Mothers who don't know if you are doing "it" right, don't worry about right and wrong. Love your babies with everything you have, make the time to talk to them and listen to what they share.

To the pillars, Rosa Lee Brown, Mattie Bostic, Hattie Britto, and Annie B. Hinton, thank you.

~~~ MY YOUTH ~~~

YOU ARE BEAUTIFUL

AS EARLY AS PRESCHOOL, my mom devoted time to our relationship. We would talk and laugh together, as she told me about the stress or humor of her day. While I understood that I was her daughter and she was my mother, she made sure that we engaged in conversation and had open lines of communication. "Babygirl, guess what happened? I was on the elevator at work and I looked down and I had two different color shoes on! One was blue and one was black. I was so embarrassed!"

"Oh no Mommy, what did you do?"

"I held my head high and wore one black and one blue shoe. Turns out only one person noticed."

My mom was easy to talk to and she made me want to talk with her about my day too.

One day, when I was five years old, we were walking home and I decided to share.

"Mommy, there is this girl in my class, Vanessa. She is so pretty, Mommy. She's the prettiest girl in the whole class. She had Fruit Roll-Ups at lunch time and she shared with me. She's my friend."

"Ordonna, what made her the prettiest girl in your class?" she asked.

"I don't know Mommy, she just is."

"Describe her to me."

"She has brown hair. It's long and she is light skinned."

"What else?"

"I don't know. She's nice."

"Point her out to me tomorrow when I pick you up."

"OK!" I said, happy to show her my new friend.

The next day I pointed Vanessa out before we left the school. She was just as pretty as the day before and I was sure she was the prettiest and the nicest person ever. Mommy and I took a long way home. We talked about our day and eventually, she circled back to Vanessa.

"Ordonna what do you think is special about Vanessa?" My five year-old self could not come up with anything substantial. I mentioned her hair clips, her light brown eyes, and lighter complexion.

It was then that my mom took the time to tell me, feature by feature, how beautiful I was. She explained that the almond shape of my eyes were gorgeous. She detailed how many people would pay for lips as full as mine and how other people sit in the sun for hours for a complexion as smooth as mine was. She also told me how important it was to understand that beauty comes in so many different shapes and colors. She explained that any of us can be pretty on the outside, mean and ugly on the inside. My mom explained how kindness had a great impact on how we are viewed by others.

"It isn't enough to be pretty Ordonna. You have to be a kind person—a good person. You are a beautiful, Nubian princess with a big heart. Never forget that."

As an adult, I realize how important that conversation was for my confidence. I know many Black women who have issues with their complexion and self-image. My mom gave me a gem in that conversation. I now understand how important it is to see someone else's beauty and not discount myself in the process. Self-love is not something I could not have described at the age of five but I felt beautiful after my mother spoke to me and it was the foundation I needed to boost my self-confidence.

ASK ME ANYTHING

"IF YOU WANT TO know about anything, I want you to come ask me. Don't ask your friends at school, you can ask me. As your mother, and I am going to tell you the truth,"

From an early age, I knew I could trust her to do exactly that.

One afternoon, when I was in third grade, I came home from school, and asked, "Mommy, what's a condom?"

My mom stopped seasoning the porkchops we would have for dinner and said, "I am going to answer that question, but first I need to know where you heard that and who said it."

"I heard it on the school bus when one of the boys was talking to his friend. I don't know what it is."

"A condom is something a man uses to protect himself when he has sex with a woman."

"What does it look like?"

"It looks like a long balloon, not the round balloons," she patiently answered.

"What does he do with it?"

"He puts it on his penis."

Completely intrigued, but having no idea what any of it really meant, I asked: "Mommy do girls use a condom, for protection too?"

"That is a question for another day," she said.

"Okay, Mommy!"

And with that, I skipped away happy as I could be. It wasn't that I fully understood everything my mom told me, but she answered my questions just like she said she would. I could trust her to do what she said she would do, and that meant the world to me.

SEE THOSE GIRLS?

My mom knows how to deliver a message in a memorable way. We were shopping at Bobby's, a discount department store in Brooklyn, when my Mom called me over, "Ordonna, come here. Do you see those young girls standing over there? I want you to take a good look at them. Do you like their hair? Do you like the clothes they're wearing? What about their sneakers? Do you like their sneakers?"

I was completely confused. I thought they looked nice. Picture a group of four, young, African American girls, ranging from 13 to 16 years of age, laughing and joking together. They were dressed in the latest, 90's name brands: GUESS bright colors and the red, white, and blue of FILA. Some had box braids in their hair and the others had thick black hair hanging over their shoulders. My mom looked over at me awaiting my response.

"Well?"

"I think they look nice, Ma."

"Well, they stink!"

"Mom, why would you say something like that?" I scream-whispered.

She leaned in and said, "I need you to understand even if you are the prettiest girl, with the nicest hairstyle, the cutest outfit, and the newest sneakers, if you smell bad—no one cares. As a young woman, your hygiene has to be one of your number one priorities. You are getting older and taking care of yourself is something that is your responsibility.

It is a part of becoming a woman. As a young lady, you cannot stink, Ordonna. The smell coming off of those girls made my eyes burn."

To this day, I remember that conversation and the impact it had on me as I entered my teenage years. In fact, I recall my grandmother saying to me, "If you smell you, by now, everyone else is sick of you", implying that were I to smell myself, I should fix it immediately. Later she explained all kinds of things can attribute to an offensive smell: clothing holding odor, not wearing deodorant or even diet is a contributor. Because of that conversation, I personally never wanted to be one of those unsuspecting girls who was unaware of her own body odor. I did not want to be embarrassed or mortified.

I found a letter my mom wrote me that year. It reminded me of the power in seeing myself:

8/7/1995

To My Babygirl,

Happy 12th Birthday Sweetie. As my daughter, you have made me so happy and proud to be your mommy. You are beautiful, smart, outgoing, outspoken, and getting bolder. everyday.

I want you to always be grateful for all of God's blessings and He has given you many. You were blessed with beautiful eyes. It is said that eyes are the mirror of your soul. Your soul is filled with joy so says your eyes. God has blessed you with a voice to sing. He has given you a good memory and you have a big heart.

But girl you are lazy. Part of that is my fault. On your 12th birthday, I am telling you, we are going to learn to cook and how to save money. This is your last year before you become a teenager. Enjoy this year. You are 12 not 21. I love you and I am very pleased.

Love,
Mommy

I'M YOUR BUSINESS AND YOU'RE MY BUSINESS

IT WAS A WEEKNIGHT and we stopped at KeyFood, a neighborhood supermarket, before going home. I was about four years old at the time. My mom was waiting for her groceries to be totaled by the cashier. There was a little girl, about my complexion and my age, sitting in a shopping cart in the same line as us. She was dressed in a little Oshkosh dress, but her hair was barely combed; fuzzy braids pointing in every direction. Although my mother was not the best hair braider, I always had the neatest parts and the cutest little barrettes she could find.

I looked up at the little girl's mother who was reading Jet magazine and said, "Excuse me, Miss—are you going to do your daughter's hair today?"

The shock on my mother's face and the embarrassment on the other mother's face, I do not remember. But, my mom remembers the experience vividly. My mother could have killed me. I had no idea why I was being pinched and pulled back from this woman who was now watching me with thinly veiled disdain. My mom hissed, "Come over here and close your mouth."

This was the day my Mom instituted our own personal catch

phrase: "I'm your business…", to which I would, in sing-song form, respond, "…and you're my business!"

This would keep me out of trouble on many occasions and taught me to take my questions to my mom for discussion. More often, it would shut down conversations that were not appropriate for me at such a young age.

PREPARATION STRENGTHENS CONFIDENCE

My mom believed in preparation. She is the reason I can stand in front of a boardroom and meet the eye of any Chief Executive Officer or Chief Technology Officer with confidence.

I grew up in a Black church where a strong sense of community took precedence. We laughed, mourned, ate, traveled and fellowshipped together. Every Sunday, we were at church at 11 am in our Sunday best. The Black men of my church wore suits every Sunday and the women wore beautiful, long, and flowy dresses. I was taught to speak to my elders before church started and to sit quietly next to my best friend while waiting for service to begin.

Everyone had a role to play. For the children, there were Bible School sermonettes, Christmas plays, Easter Speeches, and for me, constant solos to sing. I would be a little nervous, but there was no deep fear because before I stood in front of my church, I presented at home.

My mom would call out from the living room, "Now we will have Ordonna, singing "Silver and Gold"." She would clap and cheer, followed by me singing acapella for her in our living room. If I messed up, I would have to exit the living room to restart my performance. I did this with every solo, speech or scripture I was assigned to, at least four or five times before the 'big Sunday'. On the way to church, on the day of my scheduled presentation, she'd ask, "How do you feel? You feel ready?"

"Yes, Mommy." I was confident because I was prepared and preparation lessens self doubt. My mother never let me blindly believe it was right to present anything on a whim. I found her lessons on the importance of pre-work to be rooted in her desire for me to be the best I could be. People would often ask my mother, who would stoically stand in the back of the church, "Aren't you proud?" She would reply, "Of course." But, by then, unknown to them, she had already seen it multiple times.

On more than one occasion, I would come home from church and my mom would say, "By the way, you will be the MC for Youth Night next week." This meant that I would have to stand in front of the congregation and lead an entire service.

This preparation didn't exclude school plays or spelling bees. For the latter, I was orally tested on my spelling words. At seven years old, I would stand across from her and have to spell out the words that she called out, from my spelling list. She would mix up the order of the list and announce each word.

"Mom," I'd say in a stressed tone, "that's not the first word."

"Ordonna, do you think the teacher is going to go in the same order? They will not."

She would give me a word and if I paused longer than a few seconds, she would go on to the next word.

"Mom, I know that one!"

"Not as well as you should. Next word: pineapple."

A healthy self esteem is the result of my life experiences, however my mother's decision to encourage my activities in church and to take an active role in my school performance, directly impacted my professional life.

EVERYONE
WON'T LIKE YOU

ONE OF THE MOST alluring and attractive things about a woman is her confidence. We won't always have the comfort of everyone's acceptance. As a little girl, I wanted to be liked, and my mom knew it.

Before I went to junior high school, she brought it up. "Ordonna you know, everyone will not like you, right?"

"Mom, where did that come from? Why do you say that?"

"Because it's true. For no reason at all, there will be people that do not like you. It will happen and it does not change you. You are who you are."

"How do you know it will happen Ma?"

"Because it happened to me. High school is tough."

I sat there quietly as she cooked. "How do you handle it?"

"Handle what?"

"Them not liking you or being mean to you with no way to fix it?"

"It isn't your job to fix it. The idea that people will like you because you are a good person is not real. If anything, there will be people that will dislike you because you are kind or because you are comfortable in your own skin. It would be a big mistake for you to try to get them to like you. So when you see those people that look you up and down, that don't like you, stay away from them. You will find your own group in time, and they will like you for who you are."

Thinking back on that moment, I realized, even at that young age, that those who dislike others without cause or reason, do not define you. It can be a blessing in disguise.

STOP WATERING
DEAD PLANTS

I HAD A FRIEND in college that kept getting into the same type of consistent trouble. She was smart, but decided she was done with school. She was also talented, but never wanted anyone to know about it. We were close friends, but after three years of friendship, she chose not to hang out with me anymore. I would call or text her, reaching out to her often. I began to notice that she did not want to hang out with anyone else either. Although she was a sudden recluse, I wanted to save our friendship mainly because I cared about her and worried about how she was taking a downward spiral.

So, as per usual, I talked to my mom.

"Is there a reason you are holding on to this friendship, she doesn't want?"

"Ma, she needs a friend."

"Definitely, but does it have to be you? This friendship ended a few months ago, right? You are looking for a change that may not come. You have to learn to let go of certain things and sometimes certain people. Stop watering dead plants."

"It feels mean to drop her when I know she needs a friend."

"You are caring, and that is a great characteristic. But you can't change people. Focus on what is growing in your life, not on this friendship that is ending. You are trying to repaint her, but she has shown you her true colors. Pray for her and move on. You're going to deplete yourself. You have tried and now you need to take care of you."

DATING ADVICE

I WENT TO HIGH school in Brooklyn, where quoting Biggie lyrics and Love Jones' lines were a way of life. Relationships in high school, at the time, felt like the most important thing in the world.

One day, I came home from school, crushed that my boyfriend, of a couple of months, had broken up with me. Pitiful and depressed, I sulked around the house. In hindsight, I appreciated that my mother took my sadness seriously and did not laugh at me. She could have dismissed me, but she instead asked me about the breakup and what I planned to do about it. I said, flatly, "Nothing".

Then she asked me the strangest question, "Ordonna, what are you wearing tomorrow?" Confused I said,

"I don't know, probably sweatpants."

"Absolutely not. There will be times when you are hurt or disappointed in a relationship. When you leave this house tomorrow hold your head high and act like you are doing fine. I want you to get out your favorite dress. I want you to figure out how you want your hair done. You are beautiful and funny and smart, and he will regret his decision. If you are heartbroken, you are entitled to your feelings, but the next day you need to walk into that school like you haven't forgotten that you are beautiful. You will be more than ok without that little boy."

The next day I wore a white button-up shirt and plaid skirt jumper over it. I channeled my inner Dionne from Clueless. What I remember most was that I felt happy and pretty that day. I caught my ex do a double-take and that was all I needed to remind myself of my mother's words. I caught him looking in my direction multiple times that day. The point wasn't to have him ask me to be his girlfriend again. The point was to make sure I felt confident and understood that, during heartache, self-care and what you think of yourself is important.

During my teenage years, I spoke to my mom about every guy I ever liked. She didn't overreact if I had feelings for someone who obviously wasn't right for me. She listened to me and focused her feedback on me in the situation. She helped me understand how special and important I was. Mom never let me forget I was a gift and anyone who didn't treat me with respect and awe didn't deserve me. She explained how to care about someone, but emphasized that I should prioritize myself. My mom made sure I knew not to chase after a guy. Especially at that age, she explained some relationships don't work out because they are not supposed to.

My Mom took the time to help me build my self-esteem. In the moment, I didn't realize that she was teaching me that having high self-esteem, knowing my worth, and being confident would equip me for the harder moments in life. In college, I was dating someone about five years my senior and one night, he got angry that I canceled our date plans. He started yelling and cussing at me on the phone. I remember saying, "Hello? Hello?!" As though I couldn't hear him. I continued, "Are you ok?" Confused, he stopped yelling and said, "What are you talking about. I'm fine, just pissed at you!"

"Ok. I understand that, it's cool but did I miss the conversation where we said we were boyfriend and girlfriend? If I canceled, it's because I needed to. That's it. Maybe this isn't working out." Immediately he changed his tone. I decided then we were done dating and he also learned very quickly what I was not going to tolerate. It was obvious to me this was his natural response to things that upset him and I was not interested in educating him on what I expected from a guy.

Conversations with my mom helped me learn to value myself and who I am. My mom encouraged me to look at myself with love and appreciation on my good and bad days.

There were many moments when my mom spoke to me and gave me relationship advice. I will always remember these nuggets of wisdom.

"Are you going to tell your boyfriend, how much money you make in this new role?"

"Ma, I was thinking about it, why?"

"There's no reason to and some men don't like when a woman makes more than them. They feel intimidated or inferior. This is your friend, not your husband. You don't need to have that conversation."

"When you go out with a man, *always* have money to get home. Never be completely dependent on a man."

"The more you do for a man, the more he'll let you do."

"Never treat a boyfriend like you would treat a husband. Treat your husband like a husband."

"If your boyfriend hurt you, embarrassed you, made you sad or made you cry, do not call him. Do not reach out. Wait. If he doesn't call you, what does that tell you?

"Don't marry a Mr. Know It All. He won't learn much if he already knows it all.

〜〜〜

"Marriage isn't easy and it isn't always 50-50.

〜〜〜

"You know it's time to say goodbye to this guy, right? Even though it isn't comfortable or what you want to do. Don't ignore what you already know. It's over. Don't wait for a decision to be made for you when you already know what to do."

〜〜〜

"Sometimes men hate to take instruction or advice and they have to figure it out for themselves. Don't point out every time they make a mistake."

⁓⁓ **HER STORY** ⁓⁓

THE ELDERS

My mom was born in the 50s, in Louisville, Georgia. She was the second girl of six children. Being raised in a small town in Georgia, at the tail end of the Jim Crow era and the beginning of the Civil Rights movement, shaped my family profoundly. Many of the black families in the South supported one another as was the way of life. Grandparents, in that time, were an irreplaceable source of knowledge, strength and inspiration.

My grandmother, Rose Lee Brown was a strong woman who raised her six children as a single mother. But Ducky, the woman who raised my grandmother, who everyone affectionately called Mama, lived with my mom and her family. Like many families in the South, regardless of the family's size, you stuck together. Ducky lost her sight with age, but she was far from helpless. Ducky helped around the house and cared for my mom and her siblings. She told stories during bad storms, taught them how to pray, and how to be still and listen to God.

Ducky was a tall, slender Black woman. She had a deep mocha complexion and long gray hair. My mom told me, she almost looked Native American.

My mom told me about a time she was stung by a wasp on the forehead. It was Ducky who said, "Baby, where did it sting you?"

"My fo'head," my eight year old mom sniffled.

"Come here," Ducky said and slapped chewing tobacco on my mom's forehead. While it was horrifying for my mom, she remembers how it instantly stopped hurting; when Ducky pulled the sticky tobacco off her face, she pulled out the stinger too. Ducky was the backbone of the family.

One day while Grandma Rose was at work, Ducky was home with the kids. She told them she was going to go to the outhouse to use the bathroom. The outhouse was a small shack behind the house. Behind the shack was a half an acre of trees and briar patch. My mom and her siblings were all watching their small black and white television when Rose got home and asked, "Where is Mama?"

It was in that moment that my mom, aunts and uncles realized it was dark out and Mama hadn't come back in. They all ran out the door. Ducky got turned around and was lost in the woods. After the longest fifteen minutes of my mother's life, they found Ducky. She had a few cuts and scrapes on her legs and arms, but she was safe.

Rose yelled at them, "How could ya'll not see about Mama?" For days, my mother felt awful and wouldn't leave Ducky's side. Ducky epitomized strength and perseverance. My mom would often spend time with Rose and Ducky, in the kitchen, listening when allowed, to soak up the joy, laughter, and wisdom her elders had. They were the matriarchs in her life and after she thought she had lost Ducky, my mom never took the elders in her life for granted. Savoring the one-on-one moments with the elders in life is the key to gathering wisdom for the future. Whether it was learning the best way to boil yams for sweet potato pie baking, how to care for a cut or wound, or how to persevere when being talked down to. My mother's elders showed her how to be brave in the face of racism, creative in the face of adversity, and kind in spite of hate.

BACK PORCH

As a Black family in Louisville, Georgia, my mother and her family did not have much income. It was hard in the 1950's as a single Black woman raising four girls and two boys. There, however, was a community of people that looked out for one another.

My mother was ten years old and the landlord came by to collect rent. My grandmother told my mom to go to the door to tell him she wasn't home. My mother answered the door.

"Is your mother here?"

My mother looked at the landlord and replied, "My mama told me to tell you she isn't home."

The landlord almost smiled and told my mom, "Tell your mother I will be back next week." Times were hard, but the family found a way to make it work.

My grandmother could always depend on her best friend, Narcissi McBride, who everyone affectionately called Miss Sissy. My grandmother Rose and Ms. Sissy were best friends. They talked daily. If Rose wasn't at Miss Sissy's house, Miss Sissy was at Rose's house. Most importantly, they always made sure they took care of each other. Rose had six children and Ms. Sissy had five. Their children played together. One day, Rose sent my mom to Miss Sissy's house to see if they had any food to spare. With embarrassment weighing her down, my mom went to Miss Sissy's back door to ask.

My mother slowly walked around the house to knock on Miss Sissy's back, screen door.

"Deneese, why are you at my back door?"

"Rose sent me to ask if you had any flour you could share," my mom said avoiding Miss Sissy's eye. Miss Sissy either didn't notice or didn't care that mom was ashamed to ask for food. Miss Sissy was not having any of it. Rose's family was her family. She looked at my mom and said, "Never come to my back door, you come to the front like you always do." And Miss Sissy sent my mom home with more than she asked for and with as much as food as she could carry. Miss Sissy had 5 children of her own, but the community never let anyone go without, especially family.

My mom talks about this time in her life often. It was often that food and money were scarce. This was why my mom still volunteers to cook or shop for a family in need. No matter how far she grew in her career, my mother never forgot about being hungry and the value of being humble.

MOTHER'S LOVE

MY MOTHER MOVED TO Brooklyn when she was 12 years old and was raised by an extended family member, Mattie Bostic. During the summers, my mom would travel to see her mother and siblings back in Georgia. One summer, when my Mom was 19, she went home to Louisville. As usual, when my mom and grandmother talked, it was while my grandmother cooked.

"Sit, tell me what's going on in New York." My grandmother buzzed around the kitchen and prepared her prized Southern fried chicken. She took her time cleaning the chicken in vinegar and cool water. She then cut off the excess fat and rinsed each piece with cold water. Once dried, she sprinkled salt, black pepper and paprika on each piece. Then the seasoned chicken was put into a large, brown paper bag filled with flour. Each piece was shaken inside the bag and covered in flour, one at a time. She tapped the excess flour off and let them sit. The cast iron skillet was filled with melted lard and set on the fire to get it piping hot for frying. A drop of water would test if the grease was hot enough for the first piece of chicken to be dropped in. The pieces were cooked in batches to cook them evenly.

When my grandmother was done dropping the first batch, my mom gave her an update on her life in Brooklyn. My mom spoke about work and her church in the Bedford Stuyvesant section of Brooklyn.

It all sounded like a far away land because my grandmother, at that time, had never left Georgia. Mom spoke about her godmother, Hattie Britto. Hatt was kind and soft spoken, and she was as close to a fairy Godmother my mom had ever experienced. She took my mom under her wing. Hatt bought my mom's Easter outfit every year since my mom arrived in Brooklyn. She also celebrated every achievement with her. My grandmother said, "You know, I was worried when you left to live with Mother Mattie because she can be a hard person. She doesn't even say your name correctly. Don't know why Mother Mattie calls you Bernice. But God sent you Hattie, you have another mama out there to love you."

My grandmother said it with no jealousy. She was grateful. Mothers can be possessive about their babies, but when you know babies are being loved or taken care of, it helps a mother sleep better. My grandmother was fearful about not being able to see my mom on a daily basis, but was comforted knowing her daughter would be cared for.

Tips for Rose's Fried Chicken

- Always wash your chicken and let it soak in cool water and one sliced lemon or a teaspoon of vinegar for 10 mins before cooking. Then rinse thoroughly.
- Gently dry your chicken after cleaning them to remove excess water.
- Use a deep cast iron pan.
- Do not drop your chicken until the grease is extremely hot. Test the grease first.
- Make sure that you don't overcrowd your pan.
- Do not flip your chicken too often while frying. Let the chicken cook. Do not knock off or disturb the breading.
- Keep an eye on your chicken.

BRAVERY OF A DAUGHTER

WITHIN ONE YEAR OF my mother living in Brooklyn with Mother Mattie, there was an incident that changed my mom and Mother Mattie forever. One hot summer night in 1965 on Greene Ave, Mother Mattie was sitting on the front stairs of the apartment building. The scene was very much like any one from the 90's show "227". Unfortunately, as the booming economy began to wane, neighborhoods across Brooklyn fell into poverty and violence. People watching was Mother Mattie's favorite pastime. She would see anything from young families, the elderly going to and from the store, young gang activity, or people suffering from substance abuse.

This particular night, the neighborhood drunk, a middle aged woman was walking by and did not like that Mother Mattie was outside. My mom heard the drunk woman yelling at Mother Mattie and was worried because Mother Mattie was outside of the apartment building alone. My Mom quickly thought she needed to find a reason to come outside. She looked around the small apartment and thought she would rush out to dispose of the trash.

My mom came outside with a trash bag in her hand and the scene escalated quickly.

"Oh so you brought someone out to help you! What's she gonna do?!" the drunk woman screamed at the top of her lungs. My mom threw out the trash but stayed next to Mother Mattie.

Mother Mattie whispered, "Go inside, it's ok Bernice. It's ok." Just as quickly as Mother Mattie and my mom looked at each other to try to go back inside the drunk woman pulled a large butcher knife out of her coat. She swung it wildly above her head. Without a single thought my Mom stepped in front of Mother Mattie and blocked the knife as the woman swung it at Mother Mattie. The knife sliced through my mom's wrist, hitting the bone. The tip of the blade sliced a long line down my mother's cheek.

Mother Mattie rushed my mom inside and called the police. The police found the drunk woman and arrested her. Mother Mattie never took my mom to the hospital because they couldn't afford the medical bill. My mom carried a knife around for a year before she could let go of the fear she felt.

I can't help but think of how Mother Mattie must have felt. I questioned if she felt guilty that this painfully thin, young thirteen year old girl from Georgia risked her life for her. I wonder if Mother Mattie was overwhelmed by the bravery in that act of love. She never had any children of her own but after less than a year of taking my mom in, my mother had a scar on her face from protecting her. Love happens so quickly and without people realizing it. They both were changed and they both quietly loved each other a little harder after that day.

~~~ HARD TALKS ~~~

IT'S OK, YOU CAN CRY

WHEN I WAS ELEVEN years old, I went to a routine doctor's appointment before going to the Boys and Girls Club summer camp. I needed an annual check up. I thought this would be like any other visit. Except this time, my primary doctor wasn't there. I remember the substitute doctor had a strange name, something like Dr. Lovehands, which creeped me out and made me on edge around him.

He asked all the common questions, "How are you feeling?" "What grade are you going to?", "Going to camp this summer?", "Let's see how much do you weigh?", "And how tall you are?" and then he said, "Can you slowly bend over and touch your toes?"

"Nope," I immediately replied. The request from Dr. Lovehands instantly made me uncomfortable.

He then asked if I would like my mom in the room, and I said, "Yes, please."

When she came in, he asked me if I would touch my toes again. With this simple examination, we all discovered that one side of my back was higher than the other. Dr. Lovehands asked my mom, "Did you know that your daughter has Scoliosis?" My mom peppered him with questions:

"What does this mean? How long has she had this? What happens now? Will she have to wear a brace?"

When we got home, Mom explained everything to my dad. He dismissed it all. "They aren't going to do any surgery on her. Absolutely not. She doesn't need it," he growled.

My mom calmly told him that he was going to go to the specialist appointment with us to see the x-rays himself. A few weeks later, we all met Dr. Hoppenfeld, who specialized in the surgical treatment of pediatric patients with scoliosis and other spinal deformities through reconstructive surgery. He was an older, quiet, and kind man.

During my next appointment, I sat quietly on a swivel chair while both of my parents and Dr. Hoppenfeld discussed all the facts. My spine had an 83 degree curve to the right. The surgery will result in 3 metal rods along my spine helping it to straighten as I grow. The surgery is usually 6-8 hours long. Yes, there is a 10% chance I could be paralyzed. After the surgery, I will have to learn to walk again. If I did not have the surgery my rib cage will continue to shift and this will affect my internal organs—like my heart and lungs—making less room for them. Lastly, I could also become disfigured with a significant hump.

When they all remembered I was there, they could see that I was terrified and silently crying in the corner of the room. Dr. Hoppenfeld walked over to me and apologized.

"You are my patient. I should have spoken to you as well. Do you have any questions? I will answer anything you ask."

I asked a couple of questions, but the damage had been done. I was crippled with fear. The doctor said we needed to schedule the surgery as soon as possible. We were walking down a long corridor to leave the hospital when my mom told my dad,

"Pell, we will meet you at the car."

She took me into a small hallway bathroom in the hospital. She looked at me and said, "It's ok. You can cry. Get it out. It's ok to be scared."

I remember this cry. We stood there in a very small hospital bathroom and I sobbed and cried in my mom's arms.

There are times to cry—whether due to fear, anger, or frustration.

It is okay to cry. Sometimes it is necessary. She held me while I got it out that day. We faced that season in my life together.

Years later, she told me that while she held me on that day, she repeated over and over in her mind,

'Denise, don't you cry. You can't cry right now.'

She wanted to be strong in that moment for me. She wanted to be my rock. When I pulled myself together, she looked at me, clear eyed, and said

"God is going to take care of you. We are going to get through this. Ordonna, you will be ok." I believed her.

Sometimes you need someone to hold you while you cry it out.

SINGLE MOM

WHEN PEOPLE ASKED ME to define success, my answer has always included being a great mom to a little girl. I have always wanted to have the relationship I have with my Mom, with my own daughter. My mom and I had lots of conversations about becoming a new mom before my first daughter was born. She would constantly bring up how changes were coming. She explained to me that life, the way I understood it, was going to be completely different after my daughter arrived.

The differences between being a single childless woman and a new single mom were countless for me. I was once free to come and go as I pleased and once my daughter was born, I had to ask myself whether or not my choices would benefit me and my daughter. I had to consider what I ate, when I ate, what I wore, how I balanced a career, and any potential, future relationship if her father and I were to become uninvolved. It was no longer just about me. Her well-being became my absolute priority.

One of the most important discussions we had during the time before my daughter was born was that I wasn't married.

I was raised in a Pentecostal church from birth. I went to church every Sunday and I had a large church family. Having a baby out of wedlock was a big deal. It affected how some of the members of the church treated me and it took me a while to adjust to the judgment I received. Although painful, it was necessary. It taught me that the opinions of other people are not as important as being strong for my daughter.

People outside of my church and in the professional world, would form a judgement about who I was now that I was going to be a new single mom. I learned early that even though I was in my twenties, many people still saw me as a child having a child. I was nervous about everything, how my life would change, who would treat me differently and what kind of parent I'd become. In no uncertain terms, my anxiety had anxiety, but talking to my mom calmed me. She sat me down to talk about my next steps.

"Babygirl, let's talk."

She wanted me to know that even though I had a boyfriend, as a woman who was unmarried, I was a single mother. Period. She looked at me to make sure I understood, "Ordonna unless you are married, you are doing this on your own. *You* have to make sure you can feed, clothe, and take care of *your* daughter. *You* have to make sure you can provide for her. Help is good but being as prepared as you can be is better. This new experience is exciting, but *you* have to understand the responsibility that you're taking on. There will be moments where you will have to dig deep and push for you and your baby. You are a single mother."

While what she said hurt to hear and killed the fairy tale I willed myself to believe, I will never forget those words, and I needed to hear them. She was speaking from experience as she was a single parent when I was born. She married my dad, but not all stories are the same. While I had my boyfriend, my parents, my church family, and my friends—no one was more responsible for my child's well being than I was. My mom scared talked me to the bone. All kinds of thoughts ran through my mind:

I don't make enough money for the life I want for us.
I can't live paycheck to paycheck with a baby.
I need a better job.
I need to get my Master's degree, everyone has a Bachelor's now.

God forbid something happens to my family, I won't have any support system. As a parent, I shouldn't be dependent on them it's not fair to my parents.

I want to be someone my baby will look up to.

I gotta do better.

I have to be better.

My mom's words, "*You* have to make sure you can provide for her." came back to me while I pushed myself to get my Master's degree in 13 months, while working full time with a two year old. Being a mom pushed me to apply for harder roles and build my career. My mother's words forced me to push the way she did as a single parent.

LEARN TO PRAY
FOR YOURSELF

WHEN I WAS 13 months old, my mother woke up one morning, and the right side of her body felt like it was asleep. She realized something felt different. She went to the bathroom to start her day. She took me out of the crib with her left hand, changed me, put a new undershirt on me and sat me down to play. She realized it felt like all feeling had left the right side of her face. Things were getting worse. She later told me her thoughts were focused on me, she was worried about her baby. She decided she had to call someone before she lost the ability to speak. She called her friend Hazel to come to the house to watch me and then called her youngest sister Betty. By the time she got Betty on the phone, my mother's voice began to slur.

"Denise, what's the matter?"

"Betty, I'm 31, and I think I am having a stroke."

In a panic, Betty yelled, "Call an ambulance, you have to get to a hospital!"

"I am waiting for Hazel to come get Ordonna." My mom sat on the side of the bed and started to cry. She said it wasn't a normal sounding cry, it was a broken anguished sound. Through her tears, she asked Betty to come and take care of me.

"I'll be there, just try to calm down you might scare the baby. I'm coming"

After she hung up with my aunt, my mom began to pray out loud. This was not a prayer of "God, why me?" or "Why are you letting this happen to me?!" It was a humble short prayer.

"Lord, please, forgive me for my sins, I know they are many. Please don't let this happen to me."

In a matter of minutes, she felt a small tingling sensation in her right hand. She immediately said, "Thank you Lord". My mom stayed in the hospital for a week while my aunt Betty came from Philadelphia and took care of me. It actually took months for my mom to fully recover physically and emotionally from the stroke. My mother taught me, if you call on Jesus He hears and answers prayer. Years later, unless she shared her testimony, the effects of the stroke are unnoticeable. When my mother would tell me this story, she emphasized that when I pray, I must believe and trust in God and He will see me through anything. She helped me to understand that prayer does not need to be long or full of scriptural text.

"Ordonna there will come a time in your life when you will have to pray for yourself. When you are in the middle of your own personal storm and you are frightened and you feel alone, call on God." My mom taught me to pray daily, not only to call on God when I needed Him, but to thank Him for every big and small thing I had. This lesson got me through one of the scariest moments of my adult life.

My husband and I decided to have a baby after our one-year anniversary. I was so excited to add to our three-person family. It proved to be a bumpy road though. I had to have a minor surgery prior to trying to get pregnant and then I needed to heal before we could continue trying. I was so impatient that when I was one day late, I took several pregnancy tests.

Once three tests confirmed we were pregnant, my husband and I went to our first obstetrician appointment. Thrilled, we sat and waited for our doctor. We did a sonogram and the technician asked, "Do you know you have fibroids?"

"Yes I had them with my first daughter but they weren't an issue." I naively assured her.

"Ok. You have to wait to see the doctor."

The doctor came in and in a very abrupt way asked,

"Did you guys see a doctor before trying to get pregnant?"

"Yes," I answered, slightly annoyed at this point because it is obvious that the medical staff knows something my husband and I don't.

The doctor continued, "And do you know you have fibroids?"

"Yes, why does everyone keep asking me that?"

My husband started rubbing my lower back in his calming way. This was supposed to be a happy visit, but instead we were playing a guessing game of Clue about my uterus.

"Ok Mrs. Sargeant, this is why we are asking: no licensed OBGYN should've let you both actively try to get pregnant with fibroids the size of yours. You have fibroids the size of a lemon and a baseball around the baby. You are very early in the pregnancy and the baby is very small right now. Pregnancy hormones feed fibroids. My fear is that your baby may not outgrow the fibroids. The baby is the size of a pea and is sandwiched between the two largest fibroids."

I was stunned into silence. I couldn't speak and although I tried not to crumble, one tear leaked out. My husband took over asking questions, which I could no longer hear. While it wasn't very adultlike, I was no longer an active participant in this conversation. My heart was broken at the thought we could lose the baby I already loved, talked to and thanked God for.

The doctor looked at me and said, "You didn't ask me what I would do."

I am unintelligently furious with this doctor, but I respond, "What would you do?"

"Wait, let's just wait and see what happens. That's all we can do at this point."

My husband and I walked to the car. He coaxed me out of my shell to talk to him and yet there were more tears than true discussion.

When I got home, I walked in the cold December air to my mom's house on autopilot. She opened the door, but she was on the phone.

"Mom, please hang up I need to talk to you."

"What's wrong Ordonna?"

"Ma, the doctor said my fibroids are bigger than the baby and the baby might not make it out of the first trimester." My voice came out wobbly, but there are no tears left.

"Then we know what to pray for. We pray that the fibroids shrink." She spoke without an ounce of fear.

My mom's seemingly unshakable faith in God has strengthened me and reminded me that we are believers—the kind of believers in God that remain faithful even if life events are earth shattering or a bit unnerving. Mom and I talked for a while and then I went home. Before I went to sleep I got on my knees and had a long talk with the Lord. It started out very simply, "Lord please, please help my baby."

My second little girl, Ava, was born on August 12th the following year.

A HARD LESSON

ONE SUMMER WHEN I was home from Hampton University, I landed an exciting summer job. I was so enthusiastic about working in an educational program for high school and college students.

I initially interviewed for the program itself, but after the interview, they offered me a role that would help me to better understand the logistics and effort required to organize this kind of program. I worked to screen candidates, set up weekly workshops, and did spot checks on the participants once the program started. It was a fantastic opportunity. I would rush home and tell my mom about all of the things I learned.

One day, I came home upset. I saw something inappropriate happen to a friend. I saw a young man walk up behind my friend, watched him give her a slow hug, pressed his body against hers in the way you would slow dance at a party. He whispered in her ear. She pushed out of his arms and walked away. She later told me that he said, "I'm not too young for you." I was so disappointed in him and uncomfortable for my friend.

My mom sat me down and asked, "What did you do about it?"

I panicked because I knew my mom, as an Equal Employment Opportunity Specialist who gave trainings on this topic, would not be satisfied with my answer.

"Nothing Ma. I wasn't close enough to stop it. She stopped it."

"Then what happened?"

"Nothing." As my mom stared at me, I started to feel uncomfortable in my own skin.

"What did your friend say?"

"She didn't say anything, but she visibly stayed away from him. She avoided him for the rest of the day."

"Because she was uncomfortable? You need to write it up and give it to the Director of the program."

"Mom, I don't want to get him kicked out."

"Ordonna that is not the reason you are writing it up. There needs to be a record of what happened. Unwelcome sexual advances, verbal or physical harassment of a sexual nature is sexual harassment. End of story. Harassment does not have to be overly sexual, it can be a rude or offensive remark. And you are upset because it didn't feel good to see her have to deal with him, right? Most importantly, how did she feel?"

"She was upset. She doesn't want to have to deal with him again. I think he is just young. He was being dumb."

"Well, he needs to learn *now* what *being dumb* means and what it can lead to. Ok, what if he does this to other girls or grows up thinking there are no consequences to his inappropriate actions?"

The next day I spoke with my friend and she agreed to write up the incident. She wanted him to understand that what he did was wrong and not a joke. Our director immediately handled it. Initially, we didn't feel better when he was reprimanded. We felt guilty. As young adults, we naively thought maybe it was 'just' a joke.

My friend and I were assured there was a zero tolerance policy for any sexual misconduct and therefore believed we did the right thing. We had a responsibility to use our voice if something made us uncomfortable.

This conversation reflects so many conversations that still happen today. The #metoo movement makes visible how many women are still dealing with this sort of harassment. It caused me to realize how grateful I am that my mother taught me the steps to take to address guys like this. Now, I can equip my daughters with the words and actions necessary if they should ever feel uncomfortable or pressured. They have every right to express how they feel.

∼∼ ∼ CAREER TALKS ∼ ∼∼

MOM, ARE YOU SURE?

WHEN I WAS IN high school my mom would tell me about work and what she was working on. She came home one day and told me that she was asked to take on a new position by the Executive team. She said it was an interim position.

"Ma, what does that mean?" I asked as I searched the refrigerator for juice.

"My manager said the Associate Director asked if I could work in a special division for three months as an Administrative Officer, to help fix up a specific department."

"Hmm, do you want to do that?" I confusingly asked.

"It would be a great opportunity and it is higher than my current role."

"Hmm, ok."

Over the next few months, my mom grew more agitated. She would come home and still followed the same routine, but she seemed exhausted as soon as she walked through the door. I would overhear her on the phone with her best friend, Cris.

"If I would have known that I would be blamed for the mess they sent me in to clean up, I would've said no to this. Cris it makes no sense, no one was communicating any of the issues and now that I am, I need to have the answers on how to fix it immediately."

My mom was frustrated with everything and everyone. After the three months were up, she returned to her original role. She slowly became herself again, laughing and joking at home. The position formally opened and my mom applied for the role. Her manager and the executive team told her she did a fantastic job and she was even financially compensated for taking on the task. However, that did not soothe the sting of not getting the role. She waited and learned that she was not chosen for the position.

She called Cris. "They didn't even have a good reason for not giving me the role. After some assessment and discussion, they decided not to recommend me for the job. I can't believe them." Some time after she ended the call with Cris, she was washing the dishes and muttering to herself over the sink. I presumed she was imagining how she was going to handle the news the next day.

I eased up next to her. "Ma, what's wrong?"

"They didn't give me the job."

"Which job Ma?"

"The one I took over a few months ago."

"Wait. The job that you were miserable in? That role? The one you would complain about all the time? That one? Ma, you still wanted that role? Why?"

My mom laughed, "Well when you put it like that, they did get on my last nerve." I know not getting that promotion was disheartening, may be even humiliating for her. I hope our conversation helped her reframe that setback as a Godsend. As fate would have it, not accepting that role set her career on a completely new path. On so many occasions my mom taught me to not act impulsively or emotionally. She was disappointed, but did not allow that moment to negatively impact her. She learned from it and used it as a stepping stone.

PAY IT FORWARD

DURING MY MOTHER'S TENURE at the Federal Medical Center, her career advanced from her serving as an administrator to serving as an executive that addressed congressman, mayors, and even award-winning journalists. As the administrator, she ran one of the facilities. The lead managers of each department, such as the Head of Nursing, the Head of Security, and the Head of Quality Assurance, all met in her office every morning at 8:00 am. They gave her an update of events from the day before, the evening prior, and any upcoming events she may need to report to her director.

During her time she assisted with ad hoc logistics during the September 11th tragedy, supported Veterans with dementia that wanted to sit and talk, responding to system shutdowns due to Hurricane Sandy, mediated conflicts between department heads, handled missing patients cases and sexual harassment disputes.

I would ask, "Mom, why don't you let someone else handle it?" or "Do you need to leave to go in the middle of the night?"

She would reply,"Not everyone who looks like us has this opportunity and when I retire, I do not want anyone to second guess that a woman or a Black person would be great in this role."

She often would say we are a generational people, so it is important that we do well for the people who will follow behind us. Some people refer to it as a form of "Black tax". As an African American woman, it has been my experience that discrimination, wage gaps and an overwhelming challenge to feel a sense of belonging are common. All this and the knowledge that others may be looking up to someone in this role, with the admiration and hope is important. Their hope is that one day the role can be filled by someone with the same cultural makeup. A combination of all of this is what pushed my mom to be better and work harder. She commanded respect by the way she carried herself, cared about the Veterans and how she did what was right even when the choice was proven to be a difficult one.

My mom knew if she had not done well in her role, it would be less likely someone who looked like her would be considered. Watching my mother's work ethic is the reason why I dedicate myself in whatever role I'm in. My daughters now watch my own work ethic when I fly to conferences and prepare for meetings. I hope this helps them to understand the limitlessness of the choices available to them.

I QUIT

My first professional role after college was at a company in New York City's MetLife building. I was so excited about the role. It was a support position with an important sounding title. I was a Strategic Accounts Coordinator. My role was to support the Senior Vice President of Sales. I confirmed the logistics of any consulting packages sold, scheduled meetings, sent out contracts, provided reporting, and would often be the first point of contact for many Fortune 500 companies we were in partnership with.

The Senior Vice President (SVP) of Sales was an amazing woman and extremely detailed oriented. She kept her contracts in immaculate order. Many of the younger women who came to the organization wanted to emulate her.

I remember there was a client that called into the company. He was angry and belligerent that he lost his position. He was under the impression that my company had to help him and that he could speak to everyone as though they were under him. His second call to the company he cursed at one of the young women that answered the phones. The SVP of Sales called him back. Up until then, I had never seen a woman professionally *handle* someone before. It was an experience.

I could only hear one side of the conversation, but it went something like this.

"Good morning this is Rita, Senior Vice President here at Consulting Inc. I understand you called earlier and spoke with Alexa here at the office. Yes, I understand you are no longer with Bear Stearns and you will be looking for a new role. Well here at Consulting Inc. we teach you how to market yourself for your new role. And I must tell you that you have not represented yourself well today... Yes, I understand that this must be a hard time for you, however when you treat people with respect, you are more likely to effectively express yourself. Our company will not be able to assist you in your search if you speak to anyone else here the way you previously spoke to Alexa... Yes, I understand...Yes, I will pass along your apologies. Have a great day."

I was in awe.

While she was an absolute force, she was not without her faults. She was an intense person and it often felt like her success defined her so she had no patience for mistakes or lack of attention to detail. While she would stand up for others and show care towards colleagues, she could be harsh and unaware of her own actions when she was in focus mode. I admired her, yet she stressed me out because every little thing was a big deal and I wanted to be great at my role as well.

One day I was on a call with one of her clients and she had a sheet of paper in her hand that she wanted to talk to me about. I did not place the client on hold because he was wrapping up his request. My SVP lost her patience waiting for the call to close, tossed the paper on my desk, walked away, and said,

"Ordonna, see me about this."

I was on fire! I couldn't believe she tossed anything at me, so after my call, I grabbed my bag and left the building. I immediately called my mom.

"Ma, I need to talk to my friend not my mom."

"O—k," she slowly responded.

I replayed the incident for my mom, and shouted, "Who does she think she is Ma?! I don't need this job. She can't throw paper at me. I will quit this job today."

"Ordonna, Ordonna," my mom said in her calm, soothing voice.

I continued to ramble, "So if I got tired of her, I can just toss things at her… that's acceptable behavior now?! This is garbage! You can't just treat people any way you want to. Do you think she did that because I'm Black?"

"Ordonna," she repeated.

"Yea?"

"You cannot run away from your problems."

"Ma! I'm not running! I will go up there and quit right now!"

"That is not what I mean, you have to go back and deal with her."

"What?! Why?"

"No one should throw anything at you, and you have to tell her that—calmly. There will be other VP's just like her at every job you have. You are going to have to learn how to tell people what you will and won't accept. Don't say it now because you are angry, but before the day is over, tell her you would like to talk to her."

"Do I have to?"

"Yes, you do or you will find yourself quitting often and that's no way to live Ordonna. Call me back and tell me what she says. I love you babygirl."

I took a ten minute walk then returned to my desk. I didn't ask Rita what she needed because I wasn't ready to talk to her. I waited about an hour and then I asked her what she needed. "Oh, I already handled it.".

I said, "Please let me know when you have a moment. I need to talk with you." "No problem, I'll come out in a few minutes."

She was no longer annoyed and was back to her normal self. Her day was hectic and she never circled back with me. I was eating lunch alone in our staff room when she walked in for water.

"Rita, do you have a minute?" I asked.

"Oh sorry, sure. I forgot to come to talk to you."

"Earlier today, I was on the phone with Credit Suisse's Human Resources team and you threw a paper on my desk." I paused to gauge her reaction. She stood there waiting for me to continue. Unphased, unbothered. "Rita, I can't work that way. You can't throw things at my desk in frustration. I want us to work well together."

"Oh, I hope I didn't offend you. You know, years ago, here at the office we did an assessment of how we all work. The assessment aligned each person with a specific animal based on their characteristics. For example, an owl is quiet or observant, a fox is funny or charismatic and tiger attacks each task. One guess, what I was?"

"A tiger." I replied in a monotone voice, unmoved by her story.

"Exactly!" she happily nodded. "I attack each situation and move on to the next task. I didn't mean to offend. I guess you can't teach an old dog new tricks."

I took a deep breath and said, "So you won't throw papers anymore?" I am not sure if she thought I didn't understand her story. I understood completely and I did not care. I only wanted to be heard and respected.

"I won't." She turned and left the lunch room.

I'm glad I spoke to her because even if Rita didn't apologize or did not know I almost quit that day, there were indeed tougher VP's and CEO's in my future roles that I now knew how to communicate with.

When I called my mom to tell her how the talk went she shared a similar experience:

It was her second position as a Program Assistant in a hospital with the federal government. Her boss had thrown a file on her desk and asked her to type up a letter. She was angry and annoyed, but immediately did the task he asked of her. After she typed up the document, she walked into his office and instead of placing the paper on his desk, she handed to him. He reached for the file without giving her a second look, she held on to file and waited. He looked up at her flustered and upset they were both holding on to the file.

"I looked him directly in the eyes, while we both held on to the file."

"Ma, no you didn't?" I smiled and listened.

"Of course I did. I said, Frank, I don't know what happened this morning before you got here, but you are taking it out on me. Please don't. I would never throw anything at your desk."

"What did he say?"

"Nothing, I turned around and left his office."

I learned more from my mom on how to navigate within the business world than I did in my Business Management classes. She taught me how to manage up, negotiate a higher salary, and how to assert myself and still be graceful.

"Never make your boss look bad. Even if you are smarter than your boss, never make your boss look bad publicly."

"When you know you are qualified for a raise or a bonus. Be prepared with evidence. Keep a file of accomplishments, emailed accolades, new processes you've implemented and achievements for your performance appraisals."

"When a recruiter calls you and asks what range salary you are looking for, round your salary up and add your bonus to that number. Round up that number and that is your minimum asking salary."

Example: You make 46k your bonus is 5k. Your asking range should be no lower than 60k.

"If you have to work with two executives, do not talk about one executive with the other. They will trust and respect you more for it."

"You can be persuasive without asking for something directly. You need to learn how to ask leading questions. Guide someone to the realization you want."

"Be indispensable at work. Go above and beyond to be an asset to your company. Be deliberate."

"You can learn from bad managers and good managers. Bad ones can teach you what not to do."

"You can influence others by what you do everyday."

THE FATHER?

WHILE PREGNANT WITH MY first daughter. I worked at a company in New York City. I didn't know that, as a pregnant woman, if you feel nauseous allow yourself to throw up. If the baby gives the food back, don't fight it. Needless to say, I was pretty green after I threw up.

I was three months pregnant and only two people in the office knew that I was with child. When one of the older, White women in the office saw me rinsing my mouth and looking gray, she asked, "Dear, what's wrong?"

"I'm pregnant,"

She whispered back,"Oh, do you know who the father is?"

Let us pause here for a moment and unpack that.

I was one of four African American women in the office and I mentioned I was pregnant. I had a Bachelor's degree, dressed in business casual wear every day, and at the mention of me being pregnant, the first question asked was, "Do you know who the father is?"

At my inexperienced age of 25, I was speechless, but did not lash out. I only confusingly answered, "Yes" and then immediately called my mom.

"Ma," I started "so I'm in the bathroom, I just finished throwing up."

"Wait? Are you ok?"

"Yes Ma. Listen. I told this lady I work with that I was pregnant and she asked me if I knew who the father was? I can't believe she asked me that."

It got eerily quiet.

Almost in a whisper she said, "What did you say, Ordonna?"

"I said, 'Yes, of course!'"

"And..."

"That's it."

"I want you to go to her office and ask her what about *you* made her ask you such a disrespectful question? Ordonna, there is no reason whatsoever she should've asked you that. The intelligent thing to say was, congratulations, or are you ok? What she did was assume you may not know who impregnated you! Go to her office right now and ask her and you call me back. I mean it. She made a horrible assumption about you and you will call her on it. Call me back."

There was a click and then I heard the dial tone. She hung up on me.

The dread I felt was intense. At the time, my mother was the EEO Specialist at a Federal Medical Center. She wasn't going to let this go. So, because even at 25 years of age, I was afraid of my angry mother, I did what I was told.

I knocked on my co-worker's office door and asked if we could talk. With more confidence than I felt, I took a deep breath.

"I wanted to ask you a question. Is there something about me that would make you wonder whether I knew who the father of my child was?" This is the moment she knew she had messed up.

"Well first I want to apologize I didn't mean to offend you with my question. But, now that I have already been too personal, how old are you?"

"I am 25."

"Well my daughter is not too much older than you, and I would've asked her the same thing. I may have had to think myself at that age."

"Hmm." I responded.

I let that hang in the air. I didn't know how to respond to her.

After a few seconds of awkward silence, I stood and said, "Okay, I just wanted to know if there was something specific about me that made you wonder."

Author bell hooks once said, "I will not have my life narrowed down. I will not bow down to somebody else's whim or to someone else's ignorance." My mom instilled that sense of pride in me. This woman's ignorance had nothing to do with me.

I will never know if she thought so little of me because of my skin color or because of my age. Nevertheless, my mom is the reason my self-esteem is ironclad. Moments like these, when my mom forced me to stand up for myself, my self-awareness intensified and sharpened. My mother was unwilling to let anyone diminish me or what I thought of myself.

DON'T FORGET
WHO YOU ARE

As I HAVE GROWN in my career I have been faced with many obstacles. I was the program manager on a multi-million dollar account. I owned the account's budget and was charged with managing the scope of the project. As many projects have, there were changes and a few surprises. The scope of the project constantly changed and the client was becoming very demanding.

Behind the scenes at the office, the teams were becoming restless and unmotivated with the project. While I was trying to encourage the team and keep them engaged, their frustration started to show in more ways than one. Some team members quit. There were major delays, issues with the technology and the client's scope creep was leading to over budget spending.

My C-suite was at their wits end and in their opinion, it was all my fault. I felt as though I was in a hole I couldn't see my way out of. There were definitely mistakes made by me and the team. Hindsight is 20/20. More times than most, failures teach lessons that successes cannot take credit for. It was just devastating to feel like a failure. The executive team started to have meetings I wasn't notified about. They had lost faith in me, and I was growing tired of being fully at fault for matters out of my control. I begrudgingly decided, after less than a year, I was leaving the company and therefore, started a job search.

I was uncomfortable leaving a role on poor terms. I had never left a company feeling as though my superiors would've been happy with my exit. I deeply wanted to fix the project and then leave. But, I was confident that leaving a toxic environment was best, whether or not a pay cut was a result of it.

Day after day, my mom saw me grow more depressed because of work and one morning her words began to push me from the space I no longer needed to dwell in:

"Hey! Do not let these people make you forget who you are and what you have done. Remember who you are, Ordonna. You are the same person who traveled to California and took on a new role and succeeded. The same person who successfully closed a project on time for NBC before the Olympics. There are hard projects, but that doesn't mean you are a failure or that you are not great at your job. Cut this moping out. Is it hard and miserable there, maybe?"

I cut her off, "Definitely!"

"Regardless, you can turn this around. Act like it. This is not an insurmountable challenge. If you have to earn their trust back, start figuring out how. Be transparent about what you need from them. You are equipped for this role. Don't let anyone make you feel like less than who you are. You are in a role that is surrounded with predominantly white men. And yes, it is hard to look a CEO or a manager in the eye and stand your ground. But, you have to speak up and defend your work and decisions. Have your facts and estimates straight and speak with conviction."

With that pit in my stomach feeling, I decided there were a few things I needed to do. First, I had a meeting with my manager and the CEO, to make sure they knew I understood the severity of the current issues and my personal mistakes. I sent out a daily email to the Executive team with the project's workstream highlights, how we were tracking and whether there were any surprises or issues with the client. Lastly, I did an audit of any project financials that needed to be shared to make sure I was confident and could speak intelligently to them. Eventually, I regained their trust and didn't quit when I expected to. I proved to myself and the team that I had the courage and competence to turn things around.

WAITING FOR YOUR VOICE

My mom started working at the Federal Medical Center at 19 and worked there for over 40 years. Her career spanned from being a clerk typist to an administrator, running a facility in St. Albans, New York. As she grew in her career, her stories always gave me perspective on how to navigate through office politics as well as the difference between right and wrong.

During her tenure, she was an administrative officer. In that role she was put on board of investigators. This team was tasked with reviewing cases and making determinations to the director after conducting interviews and evaluating evidence. To me, it was like an episode of ER or Grey's Anatomy.

She was on a committee of three people that would assess a complaint from a patient. They were asked to review the facts of the incident, provide an evaluation of the event, and determine if discrimination had occurred. It required good judgment, a willingness to make tough decisions to preserve the values of the facility, and trust in the committee's findings.

My mom sat through interviews and listened to each person who came forward. At the end of the investigation, the chairperson of the investigation, stated she believed that the man's civil rights were violated. However, my mother disagreed. She felt as though in this situation, the facility did not have a process to properly address this man's issue, but not that he was necessarily discriminated against. My mother spoke to the chairperson of the board who lead the investigation. She told her chairperson that she did not see the evidence of discrimination from the interviews.

When the findings of the investigator board were finally presented to the executive staff, my mom did not speak during the meeting.

Living with integrity means speak your truth regardless of the consequences. My mom tossed and turned all night. She couldn't sleep. She had to say something.

She went to the executive director the next morning. She started by saying, "First please know I am not going behind the chairperson's back. She knows I disagree with the findings."

"Denise, we were waiting for your voice. We chose you to be on the committee for a reason. What were your findings?" My mom exhaled and said,

"I believe we did not have a process in place that we, as a facility, could use to handle this complaint. There is a written process for employees, but no documented process for patients. No one knew what to do for him, but his civil rights were not violated."

"Denise, we disagreed with the findings too, and we are going to submit *your* feedback."

There were many uncomfortable days to follow with the chairperson, but my mom slept well at night.

My mom told me this story to make sure I understood that it's wise to confront matters head on. There are moments when being non-compromising is the same as being honest with yourself. Those defining moments can be uncomfortable, but are vital in maintaining integrity and standing in your power.

BEING THE ONLY BLACK WOMAN IN THE ROOM

I WAS SO EXCITED about my first job. There were so many new experiences. In midtown Manhattan, we ate at sushi restaurants, had fancy Christmas events, and even went away on office retreats in other states.

The company asked me to come to a conference in Connecticut. I was excited to ask questions and learn new information. I dressed in a suit and arrived early to the conference. I sat down and about 30 minutes into the meeting, following the introduction of the keynote speaker, I remember leaning forward and looking around the room. I was the only Black woman in the room.

I graduated from Hampton University, a historically Black college, so I was adjusting to being the only person of color in the room.

After the conference, I talked about it with my mom. Her immediate response, "Oh that is unfortunately very common. Navigating through it all is something you will learn how to do. You just have to be comfortable in your skin."

"I wasn't uncomfortable, Ma. It was just a shock."

"Today may not have been uncomfortable, but on the days when you do feel uncomfortable, remember that you must be yourself.

Walk in it. You represent Black people when you are the only person of color in the room."

To this day, when I give a speech or presentation to CEO's, COO's and VP's I stand confident in my own skin. I may be nervous about what I need to deliver, but I am never unsure about who I am. Being the only Black woman in any professional environment is something I have grown accustomed to.

I know without a shadow of a doubt that representation matters. I believe I have a responsibility to my culture to bring my best self to whatever I do, whether it's my preference to or not. I stand by this because young, Black women and men sitting in the same classrooms at Hampton University are waiting to burst through corporate doors and be themselves. Are there moments of code-switching at work? Absolutely. Code switching is embracing the dominant culture or speech among certain groups (like co-workers) and switching to a more authentic self when around friends and family. I don't always speak with the CEO the way I speak to a childhood friend. I realize that everyone cannot relate to Biggie or Jay-Z lyrics or the "God is good all the time" church vernacular. It may not be someone's natural proclivity to respond in a way that seems form fitted to the culture I was raised in. However, I've learned that there is a direct correlation between working with people you can relate to and career advancement. Remembering people are people has helped me relate to others. People can connect about anything - family experiences, hobbies, travel, favorite cuisines, pets, holiday, or even movies. People want to know about other walks of life and having the patience to educate someone on who you are in an inviting way is a necessary skill set.

SETTING PERSONAL GOALS

EVERY NEW YEAR'S EVE, Mom would sit on the couch and write out all the things she accomplished that year, and then she would write all the things she wanted to accomplish the following year.

"Ordonna writing down your goals helps you focus on what you want and what steps you must take to get there. It makes the goal real and not just something you talk about. You can do anything you put your mind to, but you have to focus and decide what you want for yourself."

In 2001, my mom decided she wanted to get her driver's license that year. She took the driver's test for the first time and failed. She came home and immediately scheduled the retest. She took the test two additional times before she passed on New Year's Eve 2001. I was so proud of her and most importantly, she was proud of herself.

As a teenager in Georgia my mother wrote poetry. She also would write short stories. My mother is now a published poet, with three books of poetry. I loved that her poetry covered list of topics from young love, to lost and death.

Love Notes

I am the cereal
you are the milk
when we get together
we won't need any sugar

Sorry

If I could
find the words
that would be heard
for the hurt
you didn't deserve
I would say them
forgive me

Gone

Wonder what goes through mind
when you know you have no more time
you look in the mirror
not recognizing yourself
pictures on the shelf
seem like someone else
your body turns on you
emotions worn on your sleeve
you know you have to leave
what do you decide is important to do
before you depart this life
do you seek forgiveness
or do you get angry
do you hide from your friends
or do you try to fit in
do you welcome death
or do you fight to the end

My mother decided she wanted to self-publish a composition of her earlier work. She and I typed up one hundred of her first poems. We discussed the poems and the cover of her book. She looked at a few designs of covers, and she did not seem thrilled, but decided to choose one of the lack luster options.

"Mom, why are you going with that option if you don't love it?"

"It's ok. Well it's not bad."

"Mom when you look at this you should be ecstatic every time."

She went back to the drawing board and looked through more covers and found one she loved. Months later, when she opened the box of her books, I grabbed a camera and snapped a picture of when she saw her first published book. It is one of my favorite pictures of her. Capturing pride and joy on my mom's face was the best feeling ever.

START YOUR OWN CONVERSATION

It is so important to talk to your mom or your child, while in your motherhood role, about life and how to navigate it. Often children don't see their mothers as individuals who had to learn from mistakes, until they are of an age where they are aware and mature enough or once they become a mother and have children of her own.

Here are a few questions to help you start a conversation with your mom today:

1. What is your earliest memory of your mom?
2. Is there anything you regret not having asked your mother?
3. Tell me about your worst date.
4. How did you and my father meet?
5. What was your hardest break up?
6. How was the first year of motherhood?
7. What was the most impulsive thing you've ever done?
8. What is the silliest thing you've ever done?
9. What was your dream job?
10. What did you do when you had the bare minimum?
11. What was the best advice your mom ever gave?

12. What accomplishment are you most proud of?
13. Growing up, who inspired you the most?
14. How did you balance everything?
15. At what time in life were you the happiest and why?
16. Is there anything that you've always wanted to tell me?
17. What is your favorite recipe?
18. What did you admire the most about your mom?
19. Is there anything you would like to be different between us?
20. Do you know how much I love you?

ACKNOWLEDGMENTS

I'd like to thank my mother for always making time to talk with me and show me that no dream is too big or too small. Whether she was encouraging me to sing for hire, take my PMP exam again or write my first book, she has always been my rock and I appreciate her.

Keena, Darnella and Nedra, for believing in me and checking in on my progress.

A warm thanks to Brett Mobley for reviewing my first draft.

A special thank you to Jovan Brown for editing my final manuscript.

A deep thanks to my family for their love and support.

Lastly, thank you to my handsome husband, no one wears a bowtie like you. My baby girls, Adriana and Ava, you both inspire me to be the best I can be.

ABOUT THE AUTHOR

Ordonna Sargeant lives with her two amazing daughters and her loving husband in the beautiful borough of Brooklyn, New York.

Whether she is saving projects at work or writing down her next goal, Ordonna loves to encourage others. *Conversations with Mom* was written to encourage mothers to continue talking with their children, share disappointments, and disclose triumphs to teach lessons learned from heartbreaks and victories.

Ordonna's mother taught her that she doesn't have to be loud to be heard, ruthless to be effective or obnoxious to be seen. She wrote *Conversations with Mom* for the mothers that often think "Am I doing this right?"

There is no handbook on how to be a mom or how to navigate the tough conversations. It all begins with a willingness to talk.